To my loving wife, Angela, and to my son, Joseph.

In memory of Joseph N. Hyde and James O. Lee who were Bible Patrol Men in their own way.

To my late grandmother Doris Blair Gordon, who gave me my start in the Word of God. They all believed in me.

WHO? WHAT? WHEN? WHERE?
Published by
Watersprings Media House, LLC.
P.O. BOX 1284
Olive Branch, MS 38654
www.waterspringsmedia.com
Contact publisher for bulk orders and permission requests.

No part of this publication may be reproduced, distributed, or transmitted in any form or by any means, including photocopying, recording, or other electronic or mechanical methods, without the prior written permission of the publisher, except in the case of brief quotations embodied in critical reviews and certain other non-commercial uses permitted by copyright law.

Copyrights © 2018 Mark Hyde. All rights reserved.

Scripture quotations are taken from the *King James Version*.

Author photo credit: Joseph Hyde, Golden Capture

Printed in the United States of America.

Library of Congress Control Number: 2018952182

ISBN 10: 1-948877-02-3
ISBN 13: 978-1-948877-02-2

WHO? WHAT? WHEN? WHERE?

Unfolding Biblical Truths

BY

MARK HYDE

Contents

BIBLE STUDY 101 3
ACKNOWLEDGMENTS 4
FOREWORD 5
INTRODUCTION 6
"CAN I EAT ANYTHING?" 8
"WHAT CAN I EAT?" 11
"WHERE DID HE GO?" 14
"WHAT WAS NAILED?" 17
"HOW MANY COMMANDMENTS?" 20
"WHICH DAY IS THE SABBATH?" 24
"WHERE IS THE THIEF?" 27
"WHAT SECRET?" 30
"WHAT IS THE MARK?" 33
SIN QUESTION: "WHO STARTED IT?" 38
BIBLE STUDY HELP 45
CONNECT WITH AUTHOR 59

Bible Study 101
Always pray first for understanding

Psalm 119:105 Thy word is a lamp unto my feet,
and a light unto my path.

Proverbs 30:5-6 Every word of God is pure:
he is a shield unto them that put their trust in him.
Add thou not unto his words, lest he reprove thee,
and thou be found a liar.

1Peter 1:25 But the word of the Lord endureth for ever.
And this is the word which by the gospel is preached unto you.

Romans 5:8 But God commendeth his love toward us, in that,
while we were yet sinners, Christ died for us.

Hebrews 7:25 Wherefore he is able also to save them
to the uttermost that come unto God by him,
seeing he ever liveth to make intercession for them.

John 14:15 If ye love me, keep my commandments.

Joshua 24:15 And if it seems evil unto you to serve the LORD,
choose you this day whom ye will serve; whether the gods
which your fathers served that were on the other side of the flood,
or the gods of the Amorites, in whose land ye dwell:
but as for me and my house, we will serve the LORD.

Acknowledgments

I wish to thank the creator of my life, the Godhead, for giving me the ability to publish this book.

I would like to thank Pastor and Mrs. Louis Torres of the Mission College of Evangelism for my training which enabled me to become the Bible Patrol Man. It was Pastor Torres who encouraged the class of 2000 to write books.

I am blessed to have spiritual mentors like Pastor and Mrs. Robert Mann. I want to thank you for believing in me and for your encouraging words. Pastor Mann, "Thank you for the late-night talks."

There are some people who will stay on you until you get the job done. Joe Mitchell, founder and president of joemitchell.org – and author, is that kind of guy. Thank you, Joe Mitchell, it's done!

It is a privilege to have Pastor Sylister Jackson who has worn many hats to be a part of my team. He has allowed me to sit at his feet on numerous occasions. I was so elated when he agreed to pen the Foreword for this book. Thank you, Pastor Jackson.

Each book needs an editor. The Lord has blessed me with one whom I can call on anytime, Mrs. Brenda Cowan, retired teacher. Thank you, you have worked hard. Thank you again.

To my family, Angela and Joseph, words cannot describe how much I thank you for your help. Only you know how many times I started and stopped. Thank you for being the best wife and son a guy could ask for. Love you!

Foreword

We are living in a world where people have more questions than answers. They range from the frivolous to the serious; from the mundane to the spiritual. Some questions can be and are answered by many. However, some answers help, and others hurt.

Some are from personal experience and some are from authoritative sources. Some answers speak to the "now" and others speak to eternal values.

This book comes at a very critical time in history. It is intended to give short and accurate answers to some of the most serious questions on the minds of people today as to the *"who"*, *"what"*, *"when"* and *"where"* of some of the most vital issues facing the Christian world. The unique thing about this book is that it speaks from the most authoritative source there is: The Bible.

As I read this manuscript I immediately saw that it was looking beyond the here and now through the eyes of one who has all the correct answers. The correct answers are not based on opinions or traditions or societies' views but on the unfailing word of God, the Bible, which liveth and abideth forever. The answers are firmly rooted in a "thus saith the Lord" as found in the Holy Bible which is our final authority.

I hope that each reader will find in the pages of this book a greater appreciation for the Bible and the things of eternal worth. Also remember that Satan is determined to try every device possible to keep souls in darkness and blind the minds to the perils of the times in which we are living.

Sylister J. Jackson

Retired pastor of 48 years

Introduction

Since the start of time people have been asking questions.

"Who? what? where? when?" They are known as the four "w's" some of which you may have used yourself.

We are plagued with this thing called sin and people all around are asking questions about it. Who started it? Where did it come from? What can I do about it? When will it end?

The goal of this book is to answer these questions and more that have come to the Bible Patrol Man from people just like you. People are very reluctant about who they get their answers from, but by you reading this book, you can be assured that you are getting a solid biblically based answer. Answers from this book have led hundreds to be a part of the family of God.

The Bible Patrol Man has travelled a lot and has heard some of the biblical answers that have been given by the devil's "tail"-Isaiah 9:15. This has plagued me for some time so I decided it was time to act upon what Pastor Torres told us in class "write a book" so here you have it. Questions are coming in everyday from people looking for answers. So be sure to look for the next book.

All Bible verses in this book are from the King James Version.

The bold writings are the inspired words of the author.

WHO? WHAT? WHEN? WHERE?

Question 1:

"Can I Eat Anything?"

1

"Can I Eat Anything?"

Acts 10:15 -*"And the voice spake unto him again the second time, What God hath cleansed, that call not thou common."*

This is one of the scriptures people use to support their argument that they can eat anything.

Peter on the housetop praying – vs. 9
Got hungry/fell into a trance (vision) – vs. 10
Heaven open/great sheet – vs. 11
Different animals – vs. 12
Voice, rise kill and eat – vs. 13
Not so/Common or unclean – vs. 14
"What God hath cleansed, that call not thou common" – vs. 15
Went back to heaven – vs. 16

The chapter starts with a man by the name of Cornelius (a Gentile) *"one that feared God"* who was in a vision when he saw the Lord. The Lord told him that He heard his prayer. The Lord told him to send men to Joppa to one Simon Peter and he will come and tell you what to do.

Before the men got to Peter (a Jew), he was up on the housetop praying, and while praying he got hungry. While waiting for them to get food ready he fell into a vision (like Cornelius). He saw heaven open and a sheet with different kinds of animals was let down. The next thing he heard was *"rise, kill and eat"* (Peter was hungry, so the Lord is using food to make a point). Peter's response was *"Not so, Lord; for I have never eaten anything that is common or unclean."*

Why do you think Peter uses these two words *"common or unclean"*? Let's look at the two meanings.

Common

1) common; 2) common i.e. ordinary, belonging to generality; 2a) by the Jews, unhallowed, profane, Levitically unclean

Unclean

1) not cleansed, unclean; 1a) in a ceremonial sense: that which must be abstained from according to the Levitical law; 1b) in a moral sense: unclean in thought and life

Peter knew about Leviticus Chapter 11 which lists clean and unclean animals. When he looked at the sheet from heaven he saw animals that were not to be eaten. That is why he responded, "Not so, Lord."

The Lord responded, "What God hath cleansed, *that* call not thou common." (This is where a lot of people get hung up.)

Remember that the Lord is trying to give Cornelius (a Gentile) an answer to his prayer, and He told him to send for Peter (a Jew). Peter thought that he should not keep company with anyone but his kind (vs. 28). God uses objects to teach us lessons, remember Peter was hungry, so He used food. (Think back over your life, what has God used to get your attention.) Peter got the message, hope you did.

As we have seen this chapter has nothing to do with what we eat but how we deal with one other. We all were created by God and are all equal in His sight. So, the next time you want to look down on someone that God *"hath cleansed"* remember Jesus died for them too.

MARK HYDE

Question 2:
"What Can I Eat?"

2

"What Can I Eat?"

Matthew 15:11 – "Not that which goeth into the mouth defileth a man; but that which cometh out of the mouth, this defileth a man."

This is another scripture people use to support their argument that they can eat anything.

If we read this passage very carefully starting at verse one, we will see some key points:

Accused of breaking tradition – vs. 2
Not washing hands – vs. 2
Eating bread – vs. 2
Vain worship – vs. 9
Defileth a man – vs. 11

First, we must identify the problem. The problem was breaking a tradition - (any kind of teaching, written or spoken, handed down from generation to generation) in this case it was man-made – "of the elders."

The tradition was washing hands, the scribes and Pharisees were not concerned about what the disciples were eating, but what they did not do before they ate; "they washed not their hands."

So often we focus on man-made traditions and put God's Word to the side. This was Jesus' concern – vs. 3 and it ought to be ours.

Jesus is interested in our worship. True worship involves being obedient to the ten commandments of God (Exodus 20:3-17). We can get caught in our traditions and think they are of God, even trying to force others to keep them, but we are actually worshipping in vain – vs. 9.

Jesus answered their question by saying this "Not that which goeth into the mouth defileth a man; but that which cometh out of the mouth, this defileth a man" - vs. 11. This is where a lot of people get hung up.

I like Jesus because He always makes Himself clear. Listen to what He says that defileth a man *"For out of the heart proceed evil thoughts, murders, adulteries, fornications, thefts, false witness, blasphemies"* – vs. 19. These can actually keep you out of the Kingdom.

"These are the things which defile a man: <u>but to eat with unwashen hands defileth not a man</u>" – vs. 20.

As we have seen this chapter is not dealing with eating, but with "hand washing." Is washing our hands important?

Yes! Please don't let tradition keep you out of God's Kingdom.

Question 3:
"Where Did He Go?"

3

"Where Did He Go?"

2 Corinthians 5:8 - *"We are confident, I say, and willing rather to be absent from the body, and to be present with the Lord."* This is one of the scriptures people use to support their argument that you go to heaven when you die.

This is a very sensitive one for me. On July 24, 2013, my dad went to sleep. Sleep on until...

People would use this passage to say their loved ones are in heaven upon death. Let's look at some key points:

Ecclesiastes 9:5 - *"For the living know that they shall die: but the dead know not anything, neither have they any more a reward; for the memory of them is forgotten."*

"The dead know not anything." The dead would not know anything if they were in heaven. Heaven is a reward. Dead people can't receive a reward.

Ecclesiastes 12:7 - *"Then shall the dust return to the earth as it was: and the spirit shall return unto God who gave it."* Humans are made up of two things, Dust and Breath (spirit).

Genesis 2:7, Job 27:3 - Upon death, the above tells us what happens. Individuals are stuck on the part that says, *"the spirit shall return unto God."* We must remember that human beings can't exist without dust and breath (spirit) so the *"spirit"* alone in heaven is not a human being - **James 2:26.**

Now back to our original text, Paul is not saying when you die you go to heaven. Remember he is also the one who wrote 1 Cor. 15:51-57 and 1 Thess. 4:13-18. Yes, he is talking about our heavenly home and he would love to be there right away, but he knows that we must wait, that is why he uses the word *"rather."* Where would you rather be, on earth or in heaven? Paul is simply having what is called an out-of-body experience. Have you ever been sleeping and thought you were somewhere else, and did not want to leave (out of body experience)? Let's all walk by faith and wait on the Lord. *"Marvel not at this: for the hour is coming, in the which all that are in the graves shall hear his voice."* – **John 5:28.**

MARK HYDE

Question 4:
"What Was Nailed?"

4
"What Was Nailed?"

Colossians 2:14 - *"Blotting out the handwriting of ordinances that was against us, which was contrary to us, and took it out of the way, nailing it to his cross,"* is one of the scriptures that people use to support their argument.

People often say that the Ten Commandments are done away with by using the above text. There are some key words/phrases we must look at in order to understand this verse.

Ordinances
Against us
Contrary to us
Nailing to his cross

The Ordinances that are mentioned are not the same thing as the ten commandments. Let's compare:

The Ordinances/Mosaic Law - (civil and ceremonial Laws)/ (Law of Moses)
Written by Moses - Deut. 31:24
Were put in the side of the Ark – Deut. 31:26
Were against us – Deut. 31:26
Added because of sin – Gal. 3:19
Ended at the cross – Col. 2:14, Heb. 8:13

Ten Commandments/Moral Law/Table of Testimony
Written by God – Ex. 31:18; 32:16
Was put into the Ark – Ex. 25:16, 21; 40:20

Are not grievous - 1 John 5:3
Points out sin – Rom. 7:7
Stand forever – Matt. 5:17-19, Psalm 111:7- 8

I am so glad that the ordinances ended because the next time you and I were to, sin we would be out looking for a lamb.

Praise God we have direct access to the Father all because of what took place on the cross.

As we can see in Colossians 2:14, it is not about the Ten Commandments. The Ten Commandments were before the cross (sin?) and are still here after the cross. One thing to remember is that the Moral and Mosaic laws are not the same.

Question 5:
"How Many Commandments?"

5

"How Many Commandments?"

Matthew 22:37-39 *"Jesus said unto him, Thou shalt love the Lord thy God with all thy heart, and with all thy soul, and with all thy mind. This is the first and great commandment. And the second is like unto it, Thou shalt love thy neighbour as thyself."*

I have met people who say to me, *"There are only two commandments,"* and they use the above text to justify their argument. The theme of the above text is "LOVE." That reminds me of John 14:15.

In order to understand the text, we must go back to Exodus 31:18 – *"And he gave unto Moses, when he had made an end of communing with him upon mount Sinai, two tables of testimony, tables of stone, written with the finger of God."*

God gave Moses *"two tables of testimony"* remember the theme is "LOVE". Let's look at the tables.

As we can see the ten commandments are broken into two categories LOVE TO GOD and LOVE TO MAN and that is what Matthew 22:37-39 is all about. That is why we must read verse 40. *"On these two commandments hang all the law and the prophets."* All ten are found in Exodus 20:3-17 and Deuteronomy 5:7-21.

So, the next time you hear someone say, "There are only two commandments," tell them that in the humans' eyes 1+1=2 but in God's eyes 1+1=10, in this case.

The Perfect Ten – Exodus 20:3-17

1. Thou shalt have no other gods before me.

2. Thou shalt not make unto thee any graven image, or any likeness of anything that is in heaven above, or that is in the earth beneath, or that is in the water under the earth. Thou shalt not bow down thyself to them, nor serve them: for I the LORD thy God am a jealous God, visiting the iniquity of the fathers upon the children unto the third and fourth generation of them that hate me; And shewing mercy unto thousands of them that love me, and keep my commandments.

3. Thou shalt not take the name of the LORD thy God in vain; for the LORD will not hold him guiltless that taketh his name in vain.

4. Remember the Sabbath day, to keep it holy. Six days shalt thou labour, and do all thy work: But the seventh day is the Sabbath of the LORD thy God: in it thou shalt not do any work, thou, nor thy son, nor thy daughter, thy manservant, nor thy maidservant, nor thy cattle, nor thy stranger that is within thy gates: For in six days the LORD made heaven and earth, the sea, and all that in them is, and rested the seventh day: wherefore the LORD blessed the Sabbath day, and hallowed it.

5. Honour thy father and thy mother: that thy days may be long upon the land which the LORD thy God giveth thee.

6. Thou shalt not kill.

7. Thou shalt not commit adultery.

8. Thou shalt not steal.

9. Thou shalt not bear false witness against thy neighbour.

10. Thou shalt not covet thy neighbour's house, thou shalt not covet thy neighbour's wife, nor his manservant, nor his maidservant, nor his ox, nor his ass, nor any thing that is thy neighbour's.

Question 6:
"Which Day is the Sabbath?"

6

"Which Day is the Sabbath?"

Exodus 20:8 "Remember the Sabbath day, to keep it holy."

A large percent of the people in the religious world say that "Sunday is the Sabbath" Their reasoning for this is that Jesus rose on the "first day of the week." There are different ways we can go with this, but we are going to use their line –

(Jesus rose on the first day of the week)

Let's go to the resurrection account and see if it can answer our question.

"And when the Sabbath was past, Mary Magdalene, and Mary the mother of James, and Salome, had bought sweet spices, that they might come and anoint him."

"And very early in the morning the first day of the week, they came unto the sepulchre at the rising of the sun." – **Mark 16:1-2**

The Sabbath was past
They came on the first day of the week
These are two key points, it said that "the Sabbath was past" when they got to the tomb. If it had passed and they got there on the first day (Sunday) then the day before Sunday is Saturday, the Sabbath day.
Friday/Preparation day/Crucifixion day - Luke 23:50-56
Saturday/Sabbath day/Rest - Exodus 20:8-11
Sunday/Resurrection day - Mark 16:1-6

The Bible makes it plain that the Sabbath is the seventh day of the week and it stands forever, it is one of the ten commandments – **Exodus 20:3-17, Psalm 111:7-8, James 2:10.**

God's word is sure. Man may think to change it – **Daniel 7:25.** In Jesus' time the seventh day was always Saturday – **Luke 4:16; 23:56** Jesus was never questioned about what day was the Sabbath, because that was never an issue.

There are two things that the Bible says that represent Jesus' death, burial and resurrection – they are baptism and the Lord's supper – **Romans 6:1-6, 1 Cor. 11:23-26.**

Sabbath is from sunset Friday to sunset Saturday

Genesis 1:5 "And God called the light Day, and the darkness he called Night. And the evening and the morning were the first day."

The Sabbath starts on Friday because the evening part of the day always comes before the morning part.

MARK HYDE

Question 7:
"Where is the Thief?"

7

"Where is the Thief?"

Luke 23:43 - *"And Jesus said unto him, Verily I say unto thee, Today shalt thou be with me in paradise."*

This is a question I am sure that is asked a lot, I will try to answer it for you. Let's go back to the statement made by the thief, "Lord, remember me when thou comest into thy kingdom." As we look at his statement there is one word that jumps out at you "comest" that lets you know that he knew that his reward is when Jesus comes the second time. (Revelation 22:12)

Let's look at Jesus' response "Verily I say unto thee, To day shalt thou be with me in paradise." The question must be asked where is paradise. I am glad you asked, let's find out.

Revelation 2:7 - *"He that hath an ear, let him hear what the Spirit saith unto the churches; To him that overcometh will I give to <u>eat of the tree of life,</u> which is in the midst of the <u>paradise of God</u>."* Based on Revelation 22:14 we know that "the tree of life" is in Heaven. So, paradise is Heaven.

Let's keep on looking and see what happens. **Luke 23:52-53**, *"This man went unto Pilate, and begged the body of Jesus.*

And he took it down, and wrapped it in linen, and <u>laid it in a sepulchre</u> that was hewn in stone, wherein never man before was laid."

Jesus made a promise to him that day-Numbers 23:19. Will you join him? So, where is the thief? He is in the grave waiting on the trump of God. 1Thessalonians 4:16.

As we can see Jesus did not go to Heaven at his death, so He could not have taken the thief to Heaven. (John 20:17)

If there is one person who is sure of a spot in Heaven it is the thief on the cross.

Question 8:
"What Secret?"

8

"What Secret?"

Luke 17:36 - *"Two men shall be in the field; the one shall be taken, and the other left."*

This is one of the texts that people use to say that Jesus will come in secret and take His people to heaven. Let's see if that's what the Bible teaches.

Jesus is teaching about the kingdom of God and what will happen when He comes. Remember that there are only two sides; God and Satan. So, He is using this verse to make His point clear. Look at what the Bible teaches;

Revelation 1:7 - *"Behold, he cometh with clouds; and <u>every eye shall see him,</u> and they also which pierced him: and all kindreds of the earth shall wail because of him. Even so, Amen."*

1Thessalonians 4:16 - *"For the Lord himself shall descend from heaven <u>with a shout,</u> with the voice of the archangel, and with the <u>trump of God:</u> and the dead in Christ shall rise first."*

Psalm 50:3 - *"Our God shall come and <u>shall not keep silence:</u> a fire shall devour before Him, and it shall be very tempestuous round about Him."*

The text (Luke 17:36) says *"one shall be taken, and the other left"* this part of the text is very important, not that the others are not. The disciples were listening to Jesus and understood that one would be left in the field, but they wanted to know where the other one was going (vs. 37). Lots of people miss this verse. For that reason, they say the person is gone to heaven. Jesus told them *"Wheresoever the body is, thither will the eagles be gathered together."* What does this mean?

When we talk about eagles it is normally about their wings, but let's see what Job 39:27-30 says, *"Doth the eagle mount up at thy command, and make her nest on high? She dwelleth and abideth on the rock, upon the crag of the rock, and the strong place. From thence she seeketh the prey, and her eyes behold afar off. <u>Her young ones also suck up blood: and where the slain are, there is she.</u>"*

Verse 30 is very important to the answer Jesus gave in Luke 17:37 eagles gather *"<u>where the slain are, there is she.</u>"*

Let's look at Revelation 19:17-18 and see if it can shed some more light *"And I saw an angel standing in the sun; and he cried with a loud voice, <u>saying to all the fowls that fly in the midst of heaven, Come and gather yourselves together unto the supper of the great God;</u> That ye may eat the flesh of kings, and the flesh of captains, and the flesh of mighty men, and the flesh of horses, and of them that sit on them, and the flesh of all men, both free and bond, both small and great...and all the fowls were filled with their flesh."* Fowls means all birds.

These verses tell us that the one who was taken is being eaten by eagles/fowls. That means that they are not in heaven.

There you have it, it is not a secret nor are they in heaven.

The point is that you and I need to always be ready because we know not the hour of His coming. Taken or left behind, the choice is yours.

Question 9:
"What is the Mark?"

9

"What is the Mark?"

Rev. 14:9 "And the third angel followed them, saying with a loud voice, If any man worship the beast and his image, and receive his mark in his forehead, or in his hand."

This question is one of the hardest to deal with, not in terms of answering, but that it affects all human beings in a matter of life or death.

This verse is a part of a three-part series of warnings given by God to the people living in the last days. Let's look very closely at the text, starting with the phrase "If any man worship" we must note that the text is dealing with worship. When it comes to worship we know that there are only two sides, God and Satan. If we read verse ten we will see that this is serious business. The next phrase says, "receive his mark". Who is "his"? The beast not Satan, but it is important to know that the beast gets it power from Satan-(Revelation 13:4)

The text deals with two things of concern, "forehead" and "hand" let's look at them closer.

<u>Forehead</u>, as we know it, it is the flat part of the face that is above the eyes. The Bible refers to the "forehead" as the mind- Roman 7:25 & Ezekiel 3:8-9. When we talk about worship and the forehead in the same sentence we are simple saying that we have to make up our mind who are we going to worship.

Hand, is used as a symbol of work-Ecclesiastes 9:10, so if this is dealing with work what does it have to do with worship? Let's see, Satan counterfeits what God originates.

Look at this, Exodus 20:8-9 *"Remember the Sabbath day, to keep it holy. Six days shalt thou labour and do all thy work."*

God told us to remember the Sabbath which is the seventh day. He said no work on His holy day, but Satan is using the beast to say it is okay to do so.

Forehead = Mind & Hand = Work, that means that we have to make up in our mind not to work on God's holy day – **Isaiah 58:13-14.** If we don't do this, we will receive the beast mark.

Do I have the mark? Not yet, based on Revelation 13:16. The only way we can get the mark is that someone (beast power) forces us to choose a side (God/Satan). History will repeat itself. Remember the three Hebrew boys in Daniel?

Chapter 3, it was about worship. Let us start practicing obeying God now, and when we are forced to make a choice it will be easy to obey God. – **Philippians 4:13**

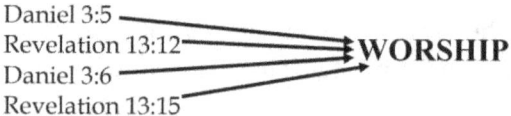

What is worship?

(***Worship:*** the act of showing respect and love for a god especially by praying with other people who believe in the same god: the act of worshipping God or a god: excessive admiration for someone, reverence offered a divine being or supernatural power; also: an act of expressing such reverence. A form of religious practice with its creed and ritual) – Webster

WHO? WHAT? WHEN? WHERE?

The Bible tells us who to worship. "*...worship him that made heaven, and earth, and the sea, and the fountains of waters.*"

Revelation 14:7, Genesis 1:1, John 1:3

Sin Questions:

"Who started it?"

"Where did it start?"

"What can I do about it?"

"When will it end?"

Sin Question: "Who started it?"

Good question! We like to know about the start of things, history is full of dates and inventors. So, let's look at sin, the Bible is the best place to start looking for answers.

1 John 3:8 *"He that committeth sin is of the devil; for the devil sinneth from the beginning. ..."* this verse tells us that the devil sinned from the beginning, you can see that sin has been around for a long time. The devil is the only one that is recorded that has sinned from the beginning. The Bible states in Revelation 21:1 that "...all liars..." will burn in the lake of fire. Lying is a sin and sin is the thing that God wants to get read of. John 8:44 helps us answer our question.

John 8:44 *"Ye are of your father the devil, and the lusts of your father ye will do. He was a murderer from the beginning, and abode not in the truth, because there is no truth in him. When he speaketh a lie, he speaketh of his own: for he is a liar, and the father of it."* The devil is a father, if you are called father of anything that means it started with you. Sin started with the devil. The Bible makes a very interesting comparison between a king and created heavenly being. This will help us substantiate our answer.

Ezekiel 28:11-17 *"Moreover the word of the LORD came unto me, saying, Son of man, take up a lamentation upon the king of Tyrus, and say unto him, Thus saith the Lord GOD; Thou sealest up the sum, full of wisdom, and perfect in beauty.*

Thou hast been in Eden the garden of God; every precious stone was thy covering, the sardius, topaz, and the diamond, the beryl, the onyx, and the jasper, the sapphire, the emerald, and the carbuncle, and gold: the workmanship of thy tabrets and of thy pipes was prepared in thee in the day that thou wast set thee so: thou wast upon the holy mountain of God; thou hast walked up and down in the midst of the stones of fire.

Thou wast perfect in thy ways from the day that thou wast created, till iniquity was found in thee. By the multitude of thy merchandise they have filled the midst of thee with violence, and thou hast sinned: therefore, I will cast thee as profane out of the mountain of God: and I will destroy thee, O covering cherub, from the midst of the stones of fire. Thine heart was lifted up because of thy beauty, thou hast corrupted thy wisdom by reason of thy brightness: I will cast thee to the ground, I will lay thee before kings, that they may behold thee."

Let's look at three points:

1. *Thou art the anointed cherub that covereth.* Cherubim's are next to God **Exodus 25:19-20** Lucifer was next to God in heaven but not in power.

2. *Thou hast sinned: therefore, I will cast thee as profane out of the mountain of God:* When he sinned he was kicked out. **Isaiah 14:12, Revelation 12:9**

3. *Thine heart was lifted up because of thy beauty, thou hast corrupted thy wisdom by reason of thy brightness: I will cast thee to the ground.* It all started because of his beauty.

All three points are pointing to the devil. I am so glad for this passage because it lets us know who started sin. Lucifer was a good guy. When he sinned, his name changed to devil **Revelation 12:9.**

The devil is the father of sin.

Sin Question: "Where did it start?"

Revelation 12:7-9 can answer this for us.

Revelation 12:7-9 *"And there was war in heaven: Michael and his angels fought against the dragon; and the dragon fought and his angels and prevailed not; neither was their place found any more in heaven. And the great dragon was cast out, that old serpent, called the Devil, and Satan, which deceiveth the whole world: he was cast out into the earth, and his angels were cast out with him."*

If you are looking for a physical location of where sin started it is noted that the devil was first in heaven. I must assure you that sin starts in the mind. **Proverb 23:7** *"For as he thinketh in his heart, so is he: ... "* heart/mind.

He thought about it then he acts upon it. Remember he was in heaven and he was able to get a third of the angels to go along with him. - **Revelation 12:4**

"And his tail drew the third part of the stars of heaven,..." – stars/angels – **Revelation 1:20** Be careful of "his tail" because it is alive and well today.

Isaiah 9:15 *"...and the prophet that teacheth lies, he is the tail."*

The devil started by telling lies and he is using prophets today to do his dirty work.

He may have started in heaven, but he is on the earth today with his angels – **1 Peter 5:8** *"Be sober, be vigilant; because your adversary the devil, as a roaring lion, walketh about, seeking whom he may devour:"*

If there is a start there must be an end. Hold on it's coming!

Sin Question: "What can I do about it?"

Sin has affected all of us (Rom 3:23 For all have sinned and come short of the glory of God;) so it would be fitting for us to play a part in doing something about it.

Romans 7:25 says *"I thank God through Jesus Christ our Lord. So then with the mind I myself serve the law of God; but with the flesh the law of sin."* In order to do something about sin we must first make up in our mind that I want to stop sinning. Everything starts in the mind, based on the text, with the mind we serve the law of God.

When that is done remember that **Hebrews 7:25** says -

"Wherefore he is able also to save them to the uttermost that come unto God by him, seeing he ever liveth to make intercession for them." Jesus wants to save us, but sin is in the way.

So, He is interceding for you and me before the Father, because we cannot go before the Father in our sinful state.

Leviticus 23 talks about the day of atonement which on that day the high priest would go into the most holy place of the tabernacle to intercede for the people. While he was inside the people outside would make sure all their sins were inside the tabernacle – *"...ye shall afflict your souls..."* – vs. 27. If they did not do that they would die – *"For whatsoever soul it be that shall not be afflicted in that same day, he shall be cut off from among his people."* – vs. 29.

What can you do about sin, **1 John 1:9** *"If we confess our sins, he is faithful and just to forgive us our sins, and to cleanse us from all unrighteousness."* Jesus is our High Priest – **Hebrews 8:1-2** and He is in the true tabernacle waiting on us to give Him our sin. He will not take it by force. If we do play our part by giving Him all our sin when He comes out you will not die.

1 John 3:5-6 *"And ye know that he was manifested to take away our sins; and in him is no sin. Whosoever abideth in him sinneth not: whosoever sinneth hath not seen him, neither known him."* Your part after confession is to abide in Jesus. Communicate – **Psalm 55:17** *"Evening, and morning, and at noon, will I pray, and cry aloud: and he shall hear my voice."* Study – **Psalm 119:11** *"Thy word have I hid in mine heart, that I might not sin against thee."*

Remember when the high priest comes out of the true tabernacle, if you have done your part of giving Him all your sins you will not die.

Ezekiel 33:11 *"Say unto them, As I live, saith the Lord GOD, I have no pleasure in the death of the wicked; but that the wicked turn from his way and live: turn ye, turn ye from your evil ways; for why will ye die, O house of Israel?"*

Revelation 3:20 *"Behold, I stand at the door, and knock: if any man hear my voice, and open the door, I will come in to him, and will sup with him, and he with me."* He is waiting on you.

How long? He is about to come out.

Let's play our part, stop sinning today, if not we will not be able to live with Jesus forever.

Remember every time you sin you crucify the *"...Son of God afresh..."* - **Hebrews 6:6**

Sin Question: "When will it end?"

This is what we all are looking forward to, the time when there will be no more sin. In order for this to happen there are some things that must take place. There are endings.

1. The Gospel must go to the whole world – **Matthew 24:14**
2. God's people must be sealed – **Revelation 7:1-3**
3. When Michael stands up – **Daniel 12:1**
4. The stone destroys the image – **Daniel 2:44-45**
5. A 1000 years – **Revelation 20:7-9**

These are five major things, some may argue that there are more that must take place before there will be no more sin.

The Gospel which is the good news about Jesus must be heard by everyone which will lead to God's people being sealed. In order to be sealed we must choose between God and the devil. Then after all have a chance to make a choice then Michael (Jesus) will stand up because His work of interceding is over. **Revelation 22:11-12** says it best; *"He that is unjust, let him be unjust still: and he which is filthy, let him be filthy still: and he that is righteous, let him be righteous still: and he that is holy, let him be holy still. And, behold, I come quickly; and my reward is with me, to give every man according as his work shall be."* This is when the stone which was spoken about in **Daniel 2** will take place. This is also known as the second coming of Christ.

When we talk about the ending of sin we must understand that for the people who are on God's side, sin would have ended at the sealing, those who are on the side of the devil it will end after the 1000 years. At that time sin will be eradicated from the face of the earth. **Nahum 1:9** *"What do ye imagine against the LORD? he will make an utter end: affliction shall not rise up the second time."* Affliction (sin). This is what is said about the devil – **Revelation 20:10** *"And the devil that deceived them was cast into the lake of fire and brimstone, where the beast and the false prophet are, and shall be tormented day and night for ever and ever."* Ezekiel 28:19 *"All they that know thee among the people shall be astonished at thee: thou shalt be a terror, and never shalt thou be any more."*

At the end of 1000 years, **Malachi 4:**1 says, *"For, behold, the day cometh, that shall burn as an oven; and all the proud, yea, and all that do wickedly, shall be stubble: and the day that cometh shall burn them up, saith the LORD of hosts, that it shall leave them neither root nor branch."* Satan who is the "root" of sin will be gone forever and his followers who are the "branch" will go with him.

I am so glad that the father of sin will be gone and all the effects of sin. **Revelation 21:4** *"And God shall wipe away all tears from their eyes; and there shall be no more death, neither sorrow, nor crying, neither shall there be any more pain: for the former things are passed away."*

For those of you who have chosen to be on God's side here is some more good news – **Proverbs 1:33** *"But whoso hearkeneth unto me shall dwell safely and shall be quiet from fear of evil."*

Goodbye sin!

WHO? WHAT? WHEN? WHERE?

Bible Study Help

K.I.S.S.

There are different ways of teaching Bible studies. My method is K.I.S.S. (keep it short and simple). I try to use five texts for a given topic, so I can K.I.S.S. it.

First – the opening statement

Second, third and fourth – state the case

Fifth – the closing statement

Before you teach a Bible study choose your five texts because you want to have the best five. You can always find five of your own, but these are what I use from time to time.

The Bible

2 Tim. 3:15-17 – Inspiration of God
2 Peter 1:20-21 – Written by men yet no private interpretation
Romans 15:4 – For our learning and giving us hope
Luke 24:27, 44-45 – Even Jesus used it
1 Peter 1:25 – It will outlive us

Creation

Genesis 1:1 – God did it
Colossians 1:16 – Visible and invisible
Psalm 33:6 & 9 – He spoke it and it was done
Hebrews 11:3 – By faith we understand it all
Ephesians 2:10 – We are His workmanship

Heaven

John 14:2-3 – Preparing a place for you
Hebrews 9:24 – Heaven
Revelation 21:10-25 – New Jerusalem part of heaven
Matthew 7:21 – This is how you get to go
Revelation 21:3-4 – Spending time with God

Law/Ten Commandments

John 14:15 – Love me...
James 2:10-12 – Law of Liberty
James 1:23-25 – Mirror
1 John 3:4 – Sin, breaking God's law
Revelation 22:14 – Do you want to go to heaven?

Plan of Salvation

Romans 5:12 – Because of one man
Romans 6:23 – Result of sin
Genesis 3:15 – Promise
1Thessalonians 5:9-10 – Salvation by Jesus
John 3:16 – Love

Sabbath

Genesis 2:1-3 – God rested
Exodus 20: 8-11 – God says remember
Ezekiel 20:12, 20 – God gave a sign
Luke 4:16 – Kept by God's Son
Isaiah 58:13-14 – Blessings

Sign of Second Coming

Matthew 24:3-7 – What shall be the sign
Daniel 12:4 – Knowledge shall increase
2 Timothy 3:1-7 – Coming apostasy
Luke 21:25-26 – Sun, Moon; hearts failing
Matthew 24:13 – Endure unto the end, saved

Manner of Second Coming

John 14:1-3 – A promise
Acts 1:9-11 – A cloud received; same manner
Matthew 25:31 – Not alone
Matthew 24:27 – Coming from the east
Revelation 22:12 – Reward

Salvation – Our need

Romans 3:23 – All have fallen short
John 6:44 – The Father draws, Jesus raises
Ephesians 4:18 – Alienated by ignorance
Acts 4:10-12 – Not the preacher, father can't but...
1 John 5:10-12 – Eternity can be yours today

Health

1 Corinthians 6:19-20 – Did you know?
Genesis 1:29-30 – Herb for meat
Leviticus 11 – Meat, clean/unclean
Leviticus 3:17 – No fat or blood
Exodus 15:26 – No diseases if…

Stewardship

Psalm 24:1 – God owns everything
Genesis 2:15 – The first steward
Deuteronomy 8:18 – All wealth comes from God
Luke 12:48 – Much is given, much is required
Matthew 25:21 – Reward

Death

Genesis 2:7 – A living soul
Ezekiel –18:4, 20 – Souls are God's, sinneth die
Ecclesiastes 9:5-6, 10 – Knows nothing, no work
John 11:11-14 – Like sleeping
John 5:25-29 – Resurrection, good or evil

Secret rapture

Psalm 50:3 – "Shall not keep silence"
Revelation 1:7 – "Every eye shall see Him"
Revelation 6:14 – "Every mountain and island were moved out of their places"
Matthew 24:30-31 – "Great sound of a trumpet"
Matthew 24:42-44 – Watch and be ready. He is coming.

Salvation – God's need

Genesis 1:27 – Face to face with God
Isaiah 59:2 – Sin separates
Jeremiah 31:3 -I draw thee
Isaiah 49:15 – Not forget thee
Ezekiel 33:11 – Saving business

Salvation – Baptism

Matthew 3:16-17 – Jesus did, Father approved
Romans 6:3-8 – Buried the old man
John 3: 3, 5 – Key to see God
Mark 16:16 – You can be saved
Acts 22:16 – Why delay?

Judgment

2 Corinthians 5:10 – All appear
Revelation 14:7 – Judgment is taking place now
Ecclesiastes 12:14 – Every secret thing
Matthew 25:31-33, 46 – Right and left
Philippians 2:13 – Only God

Christian Standards

1 Peter 2:9 – Chosen
1 John 2:15-17 –Love not the world
Titus 2:12 -How to live
2 Peter 1:4– Partakers of divine nature
1 Corinthians 10:31-To the glory of God

One and the same

God	Jesus
Creator – **Genesis 1:1**	Creator – **Colossians 1:16**
I AM – **Exodus 3:13**	I AM – **John 8:58**
Rock – **Deuteronomy 32:4**	Rock – **1Corinthians 10:4**
Truth – **Deuteronomy 32:4**	Truth – **John 14:6**

True and living God – **Jeremiah 10:10**

One What?

Body = The church
Spirit = The Holy Spirit
Hope = The Second Coming
Lord = Jesus Christ
Faith = The Living God
Baptism = The Immersion
God = The Godhead

Ephesians 4:4-6

Misunderstood texts

<u>1 Corinthians 16:2</u>- Upon the first day of the week let every one of you lay by him in store, as God hath prospered him, that there be no gatherings when I come.

A. Says nothing about worship
B. All personal ("let every one of you lay by him in store")
C. Paul speaking to the Corinthians
D. Paul worships in Corinth - Acts 18:4

<u>Luke 16:23</u>- And in hell he lift up his eyes, being in torments, and seeth Abraham afar off, and Lazarus in his bosom.

A. Hell – This is not Malachi 4:1
B. Hell – This is Hades which means grave
C. Abraham was buried in a cave not Heaven – Genesis 25:9
D. Remember this is a parable (a statement or comment that conveys a meaning indirectly by the use of comparison, analogy, or the like).

<u>Luke 6:38</u>- Give, and it shall be given unto you; good measure, pressed down, and shaken together, and running over, shall men give into your bosom. For with the same measure that ye mete withal it shall be measured to you again.

A. Give, what? Money!
B. This is about forgiveness and judging orders.
C. Read 6:27-37 again, Matthew 7:2.
D. Money is good, but God doesn't bless us on how much you give.

Two Witnesses
Old/New Testament

Some teach that the old testament is not relevant anymore, all we need is in the new testament. I am so glad for these verses **2 Timothy 3:16-17** *"All scripture is given by inspiration of God, and is profitable for doctrine, for reproof, for correction, for instruction in righteousness: That the man of God may be perfect, thoroughly furnished unto all good works."*

The "old" points to the future, so let's see if you can tell what prophecy these Bible verses fulfil. Try to do it without your Bible at first.

Micah 5:2 ➔ Matthew 2:1 _____

Isaiah 7:14 ➔ Matthew 1:18 _____

Psalm 34:20 ➔ John 19:33 _____

Isaiah 53:3 ➔ John 1:11 _____

Zechariah 11:12 ➔ Matthew 26:15 _____

Psalm 41:9 ➔ Mark 14:10 _____

Psalm 16:10 ➔ Matthew 28:6-9 _____

There are things in the old testament that we cannot overlook, as some would want us to do. We must take the Bible in its entirety.

Romans 15:4 *"For whatsoever things were written aforetime were written for our learning, that we through patience and comfort of the scriptures might have hope."*

You see by reading the old we learn, not to say that we don't from the new. There are concepts in the old which make the plan of salvation even clearer. We learn from our past and by doing so we gain hope for the future.

(Answers on page 58)

Where Are We?

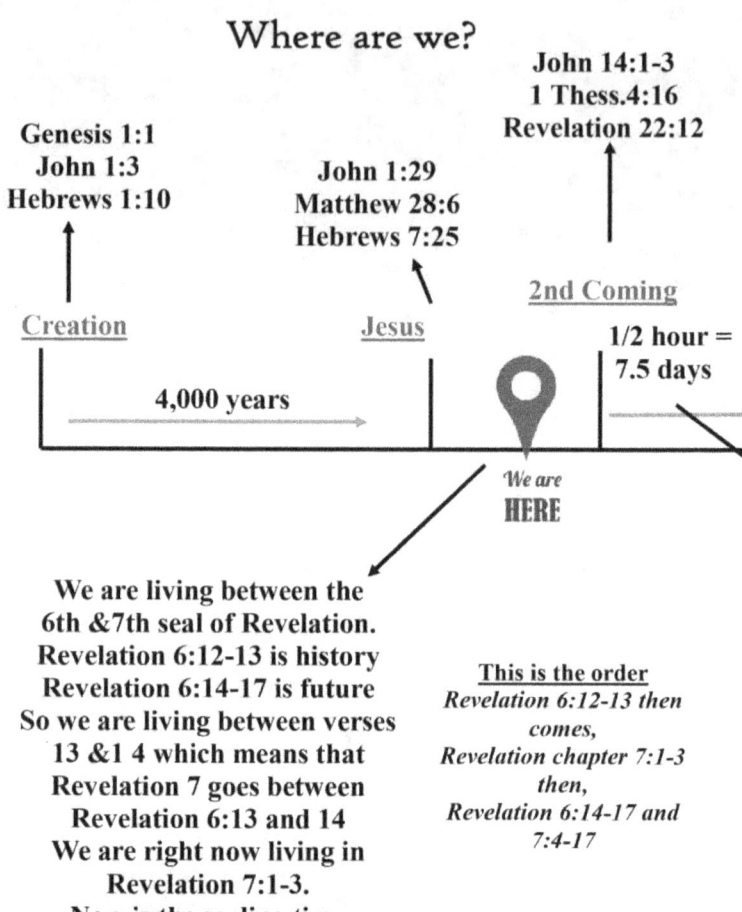

WHO? WHAT? WHEN? WHERE?

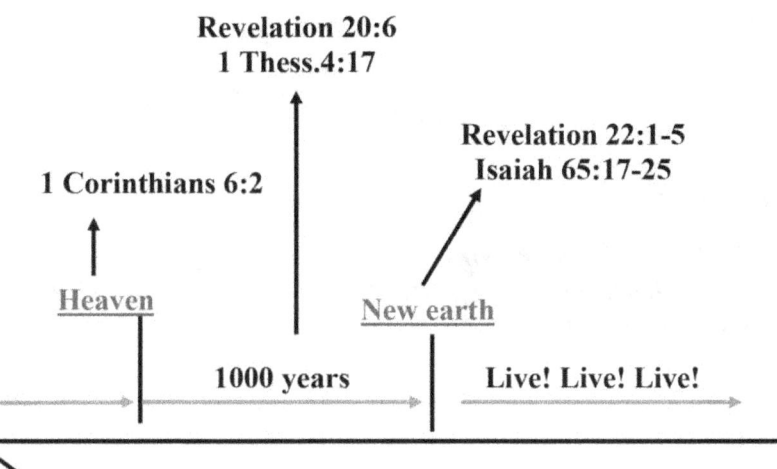

Revelation 8:1 "silence in heaven...<u>half an hour</u>."
base on Revelation 9:15 calculation
which was right on point
1hr = 15days
1 day =1 year
1 month = 30 years
1 year = 360 years
<u>*So then 1/2 an hour=7 1/2days*</u>

It will take 7 1/2days from the time Jesus and the angels leave heaven to come and get us, and we return to heaven with them.

Notes

From Page 53:

ANSWERS: 1. *Born in Bethlehem* 2. *Born of a virgin* 3. *No bones broken* 4. *Rejected by own people* 5. *Thirty pieces of silver* 6. *By a friend* 7. *To be resurrected*

WHO? WHAT? WHEN? WHERE?

CONNECT WITH AUTHOR

Mark Hyde

a.k.a.

Bible Patrol Man

Email: biblepatrolman@gmail.com

Workshop Topics

Soul Winning 101

Small Group Study

Essential Family Worship

Nutrition in a Nutshell

Speaking

Revival

Youth Events

Special Days

www.ingramcontent.com/pod-product-compliance
Lightning Source LLC
Chambersburg PA
CBHW052105110526
44591CB00013B/2361